When Blacks Were Green

Karla J. Cooper

Infusionmedia
2124 Y St #138
Lincoln, NE 68503
https://infusion.media

10 9 8 7 6 5 4 3 2
Second edition

ISBN: 978-0-9796586-2-4

LCCN: 2008926241

Illustrations by Al Maxey
Photos provided by Karla J. Cooper

CONTENTS

DEDICATION

This book is dedicated to my father and mother, Joel "Billy" (who is now with the ancestors, July 21, 2020) and Kay Francis Cooper (who has survived being a widow, COVID-19, and Jim Crow—again). Thank you for giving me the space to cultivate creativity and nurture imagination as a child. And to my siblings (Doug, Greg, Gerald, Ron, Shelia, George, Angela—in birth order with me as number seven) and your progeny whom I call the Nintendo Generation. Thank you for allowing me to be your sister in total and an aunt to my fabulous nieces and nephews who now have children of their own (Generation Z and Generation Alpha, who have known lots of firsts, including the first Black president, Barack Obama, and first Black vice president, Kamala Harris! And who have had to experience school in a virtual space because of the COVID-19 2020 pandemic of a lifetime)!

Thanks to my cousin Terri, who just so happens to be one of my dear friends; you're the best. What a blessing to come of age with an abundance of other first cousins! Do me a favor and share with your children and grandchildren all the imaginative and creative things we did!

To all who share in my bloodline (on my father's side, the Blacks, Coopers, Hemphills, and Perteets/Poteets/Peteets/Petits; on my mother's side, the Gilmers, Crawfords, Lees, Youngers). My life is greatly blessed because your blood runs through my veins and because I know that when no one else has my back, I can always count on family.

To the Rev. Brenda Hayes, my mentor, encourager, and personal emissary from the Most High God, Lord have mercy. You mean so much to me.

To Dr. Marilyn Johnson Farr: Thanks for hearing me say that this was a best seller ad nauseam. Thanks for hooking a sister up with Al Maxey, the illustrious illustrator, and for connecting me with so many people who have touched my life while in Nebraska, including Unk (Jim Hawkins), and brother beloved, the Rev. Jessie Myles of No Greater Love Christian Fellowship. Quinn Chapel AME Church in Lincoln, Nebraska, will always hold a special place in my heart.

To Dr. Linda Kalbach, a great friend and service-learning compadre, who read the draft and said she'd use this book in her class; thanks for being my cheering section.

To Dr. Betty Levitov for not only lending the grammar eye but also using your eyes and heart to watch out for me in so many ways.

To Dr. Brad Elder, whose ingenuity and fidelity to preserving the environment is exemplary.

To Dr. Andrea Holmes for living the essence of stewardship for all creation!

To my sisters of the Crimson and Crème, V Paulette, Tyna, Charlene, Raushanah, Cyndy, Ami, and especially Frankie Muse Freeman, fourteenth national president of Delta Sigma Theta Sorority, Inc., and Gloria Waters White (deceased, who was indeed the wind beneath my wings)—you mean the world to me.

To my dear Elise, who has weathered the storms of life by living well and loving deeply, being a frugal citizen of the world and a gift to humanity.

To Bishop John and Rev. Dr. Cecelia Williams Bryant, my spiritual giants who have blessed my budding ministry.

To the Tuesday morning class at First-Plymouth that I was honored to teach and overheard several say that the kingdom of God would not include Styrofoam!

To Bishop Clement W. Fugh and Supervisor Alexia Butler Fugh, so grateful to serve with such visionary leaders who are not afraid to Think Big!

To my amazing Presiding Elder Fran T. Cary, an exemplar of integrity, holiness, and humility!

To God's gift of a cojourner, since January 2010, who appreciates great Southern roots, a great homemade cake with real butter, and ice cream with just a few real ingredients—my ride or die—the one and only Rev. Dr. Raponzil "Rai" Drake!

And to my beloved Allen-St. John AME Church in Kansas City, Missouri, you have accepted the unorthodox pastor and prayed through this pandemic of a lifetime. It goes without saying what you mean to me as you live out our faith.

To my soul sister Sarah in India, who showed me how to live the way God intended: to extend hospitality to the stranger by sharing the blessings.

To all my teachers who didn't shy away or deter my curious inquisition and who each had a part in my creative and imaginative development. Most especially, to Mrs. Medah Cash, my tenth-grade English Literature teacher, who encouraged me to not only write but to "hold fast to dreams" and who brought a dictionary to me before I left for college, challenging me to wear it out. I don't think you knew how important that gesture was to me. Even though you have passed on from work to reward, I still cherish your words and still have the tattered dictionary twenty years later.

To Mrs. Patt Sharp, my high school journalism teacher and now dear friend; it is impossible to describe all that you are and have been to me. I challenge all who accept the calling to teach to remember how even a little hug, simple smile, and affirming words can make a student successful in school. Teaching has everything to do with the human touch.

This book is also for the other special people in my hometown of Kennett, Missouri, too many to name, who shared so much love toward this curiously queer hometown girl.

Most importantly, my thanks to God, who gave me these words as I traveled back to Nebraska from Thanksgiving break 2007, whispering in my ear, "This is your time, child of mine." Thank you, God, for the gifts and calling that are irrevocable.

PREFACE

This book is for the group of great young people that I call the Nintendo Generation, who can tell you the difference between a Nintendo, a Super Nintendo, a Nintendo 64, a Nintendo Game Cube, a Nintendo Game Boy, a Nintendo DS, and a Nintendo Wii without even thinking twice. And just who is the Nintendo Generation? The Nintendo Generation was born when the Nintendo Entertainment System hit the United States market in 1983. From 1983 till 2003, the Nintendo Entertainment System (commonly called NES or simply Nintendo) not only rocked the video world but changed how young people engaged in the world around them, both real and fictional. The Nintendo Generation are the ones who mastered the video game industry by becoming great fans of Italian plumber Mario and his brother Luigi, whose life quest is to save Princess Toadstool of the Mushroom Kingdom from the evil antics of King Koopa.

Here's the Nintendo Super Mario Brothers journey as I recall from playing a few times myself. In order for the Mario Brothers to be able to save Princess Toadstool, they have to conquer eight worlds that comprise the Mushroom Kingdom. Mario (or Luigi) must make his way to the castle in each world and defeat one of the King's evil underlings, then take control of that world. In order to reach the castle, however, Mario or Luigi must battle through three "underworlds" by either destroying or avoiding King Koopa's henchmen. If Mario or Luigi successfully fights his way through the castle and defeats the evil underling, a Mushroom Retainer (later called Toad) is freed and finally, inside the eighth castle, the Mario Brothers will find Princess Toadstool.

While the Nintendo Generation can successfully navigate through the maze of Mario by traveling through the different worlds, they are not yet super fans of reading, writing, or arithmetic. The Nintendo Generation can rescue Princess Toadstool from the evil antics of King Koopa, but they are helpless in the face of terrorism, school shootings, education, and economic disparities. Some are so far behind, they'd need a Super Mario to save them from the new King Koopa of hatred, intolerance, and indifference. They are the generation who has had to stop laughing because nothing is funny in these perilous times.

The Nintendo Generation are the ones who have closed the door on knock-knock jokes because of being knocked up, knocked out, and knocked around by abuse, apathy, and poverty. The Nintendo Generation are those whose imagination, creativity, and attention span are deficient and even defeated. The Nintendo Generation cannot even escape in their mind's eye because it has been blackened by a system of standardization, homogeneity, and mediocrity laden with the hypocrisy of clergy who molest, presidents who mess up, and teachers who give up on the calling to teach the Nintendo Generation.

According to sociologist Herbert Marcuse in his book, One Dimensional Man,

In reducing and even canceling the romantic space of imagination, society has forced the imagination to prove itself on new grounds, on which the images are translated into historical capabilities and projects... Rational is the imagination which can be the *a priori* of the reconstruction and redirection of the productive apparatus toward a pacified existence, a life without fear. (*One Dimensional Man*, 1964, pages 250–51)

Nintendo Generation, we must ensure that you have a life without fear that is filled with faith even in the midst of the grim possibilities of ever escaping today's King Koopa. The Nintendo Generation are those who are inheriting an economic catastrophe and deferred dreams. Who will be their Super Mario? Will it be you or me who rescues them from the evil underlings? Who will take responsibility for the great damage we've done to you, Nintendo Generation? We created you and now we plead to you, Nintendo Generation, to turn off the PlayStations, the iPod isolation, Facebook degradation, MySpace intimidation, YouTube, blogging, abductions, molestations, handguns, ignorance, living in fear, terror, hate, it's-worth-the-wait-no-sex nonsense, HIV/AIDS, stop the violence and the silence. How many more will have to die before we realize that we need each other to survive? Maybe Darwin's theory of the survival of the fittest could be tweaked to include the necessity of each other in relationships that are based on mutuality, trust, and love as a basis for survival. The Nintendo Generation have, perhaps, experienced that great discon-nect—like unplugging the video game—from family, school, and community.

Nintendo Generation: The first generation since the 1776 Declaration and 1863 Proclamation to not truly be free, not even in your minds. Nintendo Generation: You are victims of imaginative-play oppression who live the duality as Paulo Freire writes, "...as contradictory, divided beings shaped by and existing in a concrete situation of oppression and violence" (*Pedagogy of the Oppressed*, page 55). So here is your chance at liberation. With your own reflective participation, examine this book that will hopefully lead to your great "aha" and "I-get-it" moment. Then hopefully you'll see there are no limitations when the mind is free to play with abandon, imaginatively. You'll be free to explore what it means to be fully human and discover love toward each other: red, yellow, black, white, rainbow, and even green.

INTRODUCTION

It's not that easy bein' green;
Having to spend each day the
color of leaves...

... When green is all there is to be
It could make you wonder why,
but why wonder why?

—"It's Not Easy Being Green,"
lyrics by Joe Rapposo,
sung by Kermit the Frog

Kermit the Frog may have had difficulties in his life with being green. Based on Kermit's musical musings, he struggled much with being in the color of skin that he was in, and he struggled with being different. Kermit says it isn't easy being green, and for some today the same holds true. What is green exactly?

The elementary definition for "green" is—it's a color. By combining the colors of yellow and blue, the end result is green! The word *green* has been used to illustrate many things. Green can be used to describe plants, the ocean, people (inexperience, jealousy, sickness). Many can remember the first year in high school and being dubbed "green" by the upper-class students. Green is also associated with growth and fertility. In the United States, green is slang for money.

As with any color, such as black in the Black Power/Black Panther movement of the 1960s, green has become politicized even to the point of having a "green party" or a "green movement" that flaunts its environmental friendliness. Like its colored cousin movement of the civil rights era, will this green fade to black and eventually fade away into the abyss of another era of consciousness? Time will tell. It's interesting that the color green doesn't have the same mystical, lyrical, rhythmic regal power and passion as, shall we say, *The Color Purple*. No Celie, no Shug, and certainly no Mister can bring green to the big screen better than Kermit or maybe Mr. Green Jeans from *Captain Kangaroo*. Nevertheless, for some like Kermit, it simply isn't easy being green, especially if green is synonymous with money. Is it easier to be green when you don't have green? The answer is yes. Read on for the reason why.

ONE

Green Blacks

———————

There is nothing new under the sun—not even this "green" thing. In fact, I would go out on a "green" limb and declare that as long as there have been Black folks in America, Blacks have always been green. For those who are politically correct and have come to use another term for Black folks, this book may be difficult to read. I simply prefer to use the term Black because Black carries power (especially if it is a black power suit). I shy away from "African American" because for me it waters down those of us who were born on this soil (not to disconnect from Africa—which is clearly God's land). But those Africans living in America who come from the Sudan, Egypt, and Ethiopia are also African Americans. You got it? So it is extremely necessary for me to claim and maintain my roots that run deep in the Mid-South, where the Mason Dixon Line begins, where folks still chop cotton, still pluck watermelons, and where you can read racist bigots like an open book.

And I shudder at the term "people of color." For some reason (and perhaps it's because I grew up post-integration), all I can see and imagine is the Jim Crow era and its segregation signs reminding folks that life is based on color: "for whites only" and "for coloreds only." The term "people of color" as a racially con-structed category just conjures up that Jim Crow era of racist ignorance for me. I don't care to use it, and I can hardly toler-ate hearing it used to clump together various racial groups, as if to reduce the rich cultural and ethnic identities that make us wealthy with diversity.

So I use Black. And since we are in the "green movement," wouldn't green folks be people of color, too? I'm just saying... Maybe we should be called Crayons as a sociological constructed category; that makes as much sense as anything else. Think about how we'd refer to and liken all colored things. For example, do I have a car of color or a black car? Do I have a shirt of color or a red shirt? Do I have eyes of color or brown eyes? Do I have hair of color or white hair?

Back to the story. Blacks have been green before green became vogue. Blacks have been green because green was a lifestyle, not an environmental movement. And it isn't an inconvenient truth but a historical truth: Blacks had to survive on the discarded and the leftovers to figure out how to make a meal and even a dollar out of fifteen cents.

Can we just go back a few years ago to Dr. George Washington Carver (July 12, 1864 to January 5, 1943) who was a botanical researcher and agronomy educator at the Tuskegee Institute in Tuskegee, Alabama, teaching former slaves farming techniques for self-sufficiency. Carver wanted poor farmers to grow alternative crops as both a source of their own food and a cash crop. His most famous method of promoting the peanut involved his creation of about two hundred existing industrial products from peanuts, including cosmetics, dyes, paints, plastics, gasoline, and nitroglycerin. Dr. Carver also developed more than one hundred ways to use sweet potatoes. Dr. Carver even figured out how to foster soil conservation through crop rotation, making him a notable environmentalist. He figured that cotton and tobacco crops were depleting the soil of its natural nutrients and that to rotate those crops with sweet potatoes, peanuts, or peas would make the ground more fertile and yield more in organic harvests!

Many of Dr. Carver's contemporaries were also quite resourceful; some of them are related to me. The legacy of greatness and greenness of Roy and Louise Cooper, my paternal grandparents, speaks for itself. From the halls of academia, having the longest lineage of descendants to ever attend Lincoln University, to the soils of agriculture cultivated in the Missouri Bootheel, working on ways to grow indigenous and innovative crops, the legacy is sustainable. What is interesting is that my grandfather's siblings were all academicians and scholars who established schools, yet my grandfather used his formal education to study the earth, the dirt from which humankind was given life. Not only was Roy Cooper Sr. fond of the life-giving source of the earth but he was a great caretaker of animals as well. From chickens, cows, and even hogs to cats, crawdads, and dogs, the animals instinctively knew him as provider, nurturer. He knew them as well, calling out, "Here chick, chick, chickee" to feed the chickens and "Soooeee" to alert the pigs that it was time for feed. It wasn't unusual to see my grandfather cuddle and coo his animals to sleep. As a wide-eyed, imaginative child, I thought my grandfather was just like what I imagined God to be: loving, caring, compassionate, intelligent, giving, nurturing, and accepting.

It is no surprise, then, that the Cooper Farm is the place where imagination, creativity, and community converged. It is the place where more than two hundred trees have been planted from 1993 to date as a way to be green before the movement took root. Incidentally, each of the trees cost absolutely nothing. The trees were found in my parents' backyard by my father, Joel Cooper, who transported each to the Cooper Farm.

The variety of trees that were dedicated to family and friends, both deceased and living, as a memorial park include black walnut, cherry, peach, apple, pear, plum, pecan, oak, and weeping willow. The Cooper Farm is where the many Bootheel Black farmers came together during the sharecroppers revolt during the 1920s and '30s, some of whom lost their farms during the Great Depression yet still came to the Cooper Farm to celebrate the time after planting and just before the harvest. This gathering now has evolved into an annual family reunion where more than seven hundred family and friends gather and feel the spirit that hovers over that sacred space cradled in God's hand.

The Cooper Farm is the place where a curious kid can be an inventive kid. It is the place where dirt was swept away by my siblings and cousins to make a bowling alley, complete with sixteen-ounce glass bottles serving as bowling pins. It is the place where you could make a mean mud pie (by using the well's rusty iron water and the rich soil from near the smokehouse, adjacent to the chicken coop). It is the place where the outdoor toilet still stands, now a monument (or relic of sorts) that my generation uses once a year during our annual family and friends reunion, just to remind us of how we've been blessed with modern conveniences yet cursed by the loss of simplicity.

For the purpose of this book of musings filled with empirical research and anecdotes from my ancestors, I shall define my subjects as the antebellum and post-Emancipation Proclamation Negroes (that includes the twentieth-century Black folk, too) who had to be inventive, innovative, resourceful, and, yes, "green."

Through the next several pages you will see how recycling and organic produce is not new, but certainly adds an interesting profit-making component to this capitalistic culture. At the very core of capitalism is private ownership, where humans are able to freely and cooperatively produce under economic class distinctions.

When farming became big business, with its use of pesticides and growth hormones to mass-produce and meet the demand of the growing United States population, the small farm kept the organic growing method as its core. And now, with the advent of farm products that seem abnormally sized, even seedless (does it make sense to buy grape seeds as a vitamin supplement when grapes naturally have seeds?), people want the natural, organic—not genetically engineered or altered food—at whatever cost. So can we have grapes with seeds, watermelons with seeds, please! Thank God we still have sunflowers with seeds.

Stick an organic label on something and you'll be paying out of your ears. Here's something to think about: Can milk be organic when it has been pasteurized, homogenized, and stored for shipping in milk cartons or plastic jugs? I'm just saying... Place "free range" on something and you'll be paying out-of-this-world prices. If I were a betting kind of person, I would wager that even in the context of free range, there are fences all around—so then is that caged bird really free to sing? Why does it cost more if it is natural and free of hormones, pesticides, and herbicides? Seems like a complex contradiction to me. Again, I'm just saying. And wouldn't "raw" sugar be simply sugar cane? How much more "raw" can you get?! Is there such a thing as "half foods"?—yet we have "whole food" markets all over the place!

If this labeling and marketing with product information is supposedly better, then why is it outpricing the poor consumer who has to decide how to spend a fixed-income amount of money on the cheapest and to try to get the most for a buck buying bulk? Think about it. How many organic, whole foods stores have signs in the front that say "We accept EBT," which stands for the Electronic Benefit Transfer that replaced food stamps. (The EBT can be used like an ATM card—is that enough alphabet soup?) Ironically, Blacks were green because they were poor. Now the poor can't afford to be green. Is green the new social class that outcasts and further marginalizes through economic oppression? Is green the new color for discriminating against the poor while raising its head with green-eyed envy? How many of the poor can afford the new hybrid automobiles? Better yet, how many of the poor bargain hunters, who have seen Wal-Mart as the haven for savings, spare a dollar to purchase the black and green reusable "sustainable-is-good" bags? Wal-Mart, I remember when you were small and brown with stock options for workers and the home of low prices. For more than twenty-five years, Wal-Mart, you've been in my life. I've been your champion, Wal-Mart, but now I'm confused. Why didn't you just give the reusable bags away? Is it really all about the green, the color of money, or are you, Wal-Mart, really green? Honestly, how many Black folks, who are earnestly trying to be green—and poor, scraggly folks, too—could walk into a store with sustainable, reusable bags and not be scoped out by security? Perhaps they would even be picked up for shoplifting!

Seems to me there are more working poor in this country who are looking for a better existence and a better way to provide for their families. Yet with all these new regulations for energy efficiency and carbon friendliness, the poor, once again, suffer. Kermit's green song, which was an anthem for the disenfranchised and economically disadvantaged, could be applied today to this new social-casting capitalistic movement known as the green. Why does color always have to be a divisive issue...?

Maybe we should reclaim our heritage as conscious, caring citizens of these United States and live as best we can with the intention of loving our free-range, free-will neighbors just as we would love our organic selves. Here's a challenge to Black folks: Can we lose the bling and reclaim the green? Can we reclaim our roots as green Blacks who ate turnip greens and cornbread? Check it out.

TWO

Extreme Recycling

———

Black folks always did and still do things to the extreme. And by default, Black folks were green before green became the thing, and Black folks took recycling to the extreme. If it was a "thing," it could be reused for something. Remember those super-thick department store catalogs from Sears? Remember how your grandmother would fold the pages down to form a doorstop for each door in the house? Wasn't that a novel idea and a perfect way to recycle old catalogs? Guess what old newspapers were used for ... outhouse purposes (need I say more). Paper grocery sacks would be used for "pot" popcorn bags. Once that popcorn was finished popping, just dump the pot over the brown paper sack, put in a little salt, and give it a good shake, shake, shake. Soon the brown sack would be spotted with grease and the popcorn would be oozing with flavor. There was never any worry about toxic fumes from pot popcorn, just tantalizing aroma filled with the mouth-watering anticipation of indulging. Paper sacks were also used as Christmas stockings—to decorate and to fill with gifts, fruits, and nuts. It was a joy at Christmas time to decorate a paper sack—not a stocking, 'cause folks in my neighborhood had furnaces, not fireplaces. Yet in our imagination at Christmas, we'd have a chimney on the roof for Santa, even if we didn't have a fireplace. Santa didn't discriminate.

And it really didn't matter what Jolly Old Saint Nick would bring. We'd always revert to playing games we had made up:

kitchen-table football (yes, the kitchen table would be the foot-ball field and thumbs horizontally touching with two pointers up would make the perfect goal posts). There was nothing like wire-hanger basketball (you'd just stretch out a crooked hanger until it was round enough to dunk a wad of old school work). Whenever the coast was clear of parents, coffee-table badmin-ton would begin. The living room was the court, the coffee table was the net, and the badminton rackets were stretched-out wire hangers with old knee-highs pulled over. Let the games begin. Angela, George, and I would play for hours at a time, especially if the weather was too bad to be outside to play. Pretty creative, huh?

Here's a surprise: If you opened up a can of Crisco, especially if it had been sitting on the stove, you'd find old grease that was being stored to fry up a batch of french fries or catfish. Of course the Crisco cans were metal back then, and if they weren't used to store old grease, they'd be perfect for making stilts. You could see kids in the neighborhood looking silly on the stilts, walking tall—trying not to fall. Those were the good old days before the Nintendo craze.

Now, as a boost for laundry, here's what you needed: melt-ed-down bath soap that was now too small to lather. Just toss it in the washing machine. This extra laundry boost was especial-ly important to get grass stains out of our blue jeans. And guess what? It worked. OxiClean, you'd better believe it.

And even before the invention of the modern washing ma-chine, there was the use of a number three tub. Not only was the number three tub used to do the last rinse of laundry, but it had another, dual purpose as well. The duality of the number three tub was to rinse clothes and to bathe in. After the outdoor toi-let and the number three tub were replaced with more modern conveniences such as indoor facilities, the number three tub, along with its sister, the number two tub, didn't drift away into oblivion but served as intentional flower-garden basins. Sustainable living at its finest.

Of course, the tubs were made of iron, and in the midst of figuring ways to reuse the scraps of iron, scrap iron became a major income-supplement business for some. If you were to break down old washers, air conditioners, hoes, shovels, and tractors, you would find valuable copper, iron, and other metals. Mr. T Younger, a genius of a man with only a third-grade education, still scraps iron for his lucrative business at over the age of eighty-nine. When asked why he started collecting the scraps of iron, he said very simply, "Farming wasn't enough money to raise a family for my wife and me." And a sustainable living indeed. Just go and look at Uncle T, who lived to pay for everything with cash; he doesn't have any debt.

From scrap iron to plastic, let's see when the paradigm shifted. My oldest sister Shelia recollects the excitement of Big Mama (our maternal great-grandmother) to have milk in plastic jugs. This would help the milk have longer refrigerator life. The plastic milk jugs would last through infinity as well. So here's what we did to recycle the plastic. Plastic milk jugs were used for Kool-Aid (and you could cut them in half to seed plants for the spring garden). Two-liter plastic soda bottles would be used to make ice in the deep freezer (and if you didn't have an ice pick, a butcher knife would do the trick). We never had to buy ice, we just filled up the plastic bottles, tossed them in the deep freezer, and then we'd load up the cooler for weekend fishing trips to keep our lunches/beverages cold. These cold packs were also great for the sprains and pains of outdoor play. As if that wasn't enough of a pleasure, my older brothers Greg and Ron used to store chewed chewing gum in the freezer. Gum recycled, you bet. Now I know the reason why folks stuck gum under the pews at church and were territorial about their seat. (Just kidding!)

Just like the mystery behind the Crisco can contents, you'd never know what you'd find in a Pringles potato chip can, and most of the time you'd find nickels, pennies, quarters, and dimes. The potato chip cans made perfect piggy banks. And the mystery of contents continued with "butter" dishes that would be used to store leftover food in the refrigerator or freezer. When an ordinary bowl wasn't big enough and neither was a regular serving size, you could use these "butter dishes" as cereal bowls. They also worked perfectly to eat ice cream, like my brother George did often.

Here's another novel recycling idea that could be a great gaming idea for the Nintendo Generation. It is a board game. One will never be bored by playing a good game of checkers, and there is nothing like a good game of checkers when you are playing with bottle caps. Coca-Cola bottle caps (and even Peach Nehi bottle caps) would turn into checkerboard pieces. Of course, the only way to play checkers would be on a large piece of scrap wood that was sanded down and painted in the checkerboard pattern. The checker game would be so intense every year during the family reunion, the king of checkers would be all smiles.

Speaking of smiles, nothing was spared, not even dental care, when it came to organic and green living. Can I pause and ask a couple of simple questions before going on? How many of you who claim to be green would brush your teeth using what is found in nature instead of the plastic toothbrushes of today? Imagine saving millions of barrels of oil that are used to transport toothbrushes each year (of course, I'm being facetious, but that's the environmentalist argument for eradicating the use of plastics). If you are going to be green, you may as well go all the way, right? Just step outside and grab a twig to brush your teeth. When Black folks were green, Black folks used elm tree twigs as toothbrushes; and if you had a little money, baking soda was used as the toothpaste. Big Mama had every last one of her teeth and not even one cavity. Just as the elm tree twigs were used as toothbrushes, did you know that in India today the neem tree twigs are used by people to brush their teeth? Folks in India have the most beautiful smiles. In Africa, the same is true. According to Pascal Fletcher Dakar in an article for a Nairobi newspaper entitled *The Nation* on June 21, 2007,

Across the continent south of the Sahara, many people go about their daily business with a small stick or twig protruding from their mouth, which they chew or use to scrub their teeth. Cut from wild trees and shrubs in the bush, this is the African toothbrush... In Senegal, the chewing stick is call "sothiou," which means "to clean" in the local Wolof language. In east Africa, the stick is called "mswaki," the Swahili word for toothbrush. Their users say the sticks are also medicinal, providing not just dental hygiene but also curing a variety of other ills. Dental experts agree they seem to clean teeth well and some up-market health stores in the United States have been selling chew-sticks as a natural form of dental care. Another bush toothbrush, the Werek, is cut from the branches of the gum tree, while the thicker Neep-Neep helps ease toothache. The Cola, cut from a soft, whitish wood, is prized for its sweet taste. If chewed, most of the twigs fray into finer strands, which have the effect of "flossing" between the teeth, or if rubbed up and down, can scrub tooth enamel clean as well as any brush. But they can taste bitter compared with commercial toothpastes... Although commercially made toothbrushes from leading international brands are available in Dakar supermarkets and pharmacies, many people say they prefer the chew sticks.

Now that plastic toothbrushes are in the world, old toothbrushes work well in the house-cleaning arena. In fact, with elbow grease, a little Comet, and an old toothbrush, one could remove stains from soap and the like from around the tiles in the shower. At least, that is what was done with old toothbrushes in the Kay Cooper household.

Moving from teeth to tires—how do you reuse a flat rubber tire? Look no further for the answer. Tractor tires and even automobile tires were used as swings and flower planters for beautiful, unusual flower beds. Drive along any country road and you'd see how tires added to the natural landscape with petunias, begonias, marigolds, and rooster cones, all arranged for aesthetic beauty.

Clearly there was no limit to what one could do. The only limitations were really how far the mind would travel to explore new ways to use old things, including old white socks. Let my Aunt Juel have her way, and you'd have an adorable monkey doll made from the old socks and her secret sewing ingredient. Other garments of clothing, the more ragged and tattered the better, would be pieced together to form a beautiful quilt. From mere scraps of clothing, a masterpiece of intricate detail and design would emerge, just in time for the winter (and just in time to share as gifts). I shall never forget the beautiful windmill-patterned quilt that my paternal grandmother ("Grandmother," we called her) and her friends, Ms. Ozzie Ruff and Ms.

Fannie Mae, pieced together for me for my "hope chest." As we sat around the kitchen table, my mother was present as well, and I was taught what it meant to grow up to be a strong Black woman.

I was only in the fifth grade and a tomboy to boot. And I vividly remember, as if only yesterday, sitting around the kitchen table on the Cooper Farm with these powerful quilting women who began the inquisition. I remember my grandmother asking, "Has she received her womanhood?" My mother said, "Not yet!" So I kind of knew where this conversation was going—yet another talk about the beginning of the end—the punctuation mark—the "period."

As they pieced the quilt together, my job was to thread needles that were too difficult for arthritic hands and for almost blind eyes to see the eye of the needle. I soaked up like a sponge the women's wisdom, women power of these three generations of strong Black womanhood. In retrospect, it was one of the most awesome experiences in my life, a defining time that shaped me. These women deposited in me a hope, empowered with creativity, all wrapped up in a masterpiece for a hope chest for my future. Perhaps this hope chest would have imagination. This hope chest would have faith inside. This hope chest would have dreams inside. This hope chest would have joy inside. Today my hope is that the Nintendo Generation can have a quilt-piecing experience, too. I hope that I can share women's wisdom with someone who is a generation younger than me. Will you make that hope against hope a reality?

Incidentally, not only could folks quilt and imagine their way to a beautiful masterpiece out of scraps of clothing, but folks could sew as well. Gunny bags would convert into the nicest shirts and dresses. And folks would be starched, dressed to impress; you'd better believe it. I don't know about you, but I'm tired of viewing boxer shorts and waistlines, wrinkled clothes, white Ts, and backsides. Nintendo Generation, you spend so much green on clothes, but in my opinion and empirical research, based solely on photos of the past and what I see, this has to be the slouchiest season in clothing history. What happened to belts, starch, and shoes other than tennis and house shoes, for heaven's sake? I cringe when I see young women wearing pajama bottoms in public. Ain't nothing cute about it. I'm just saying.

If you want to know how to truly be a "fashionista" and a diva, take a page out of "herstory." My Great Aunt Beulah and Aunt Virgie Lee could have had their own couture line. Just maybe if we could sew again, we'd put an end to the sweatshops in India, China, Indonesia, Sri Lanka, Bangladesh, or wherever labor is cheap at the expense of indigenous peoples' blood, sweat, and tears. And clothing passed down from one sibling to the next, hand-me-down shoes, coats, and vests—didn't make any difference as long as the clothes were clean and pressed. Now with the childhood obesity pandemic, hand-me-downs wouldn't fit sibling to sibling—too many unhealthy eating habits, lack of outdoor activities, and the fast food of convenience that lacks nutrition. If you have more than one child, wouldn't it be great to be able to pass down the clothing? (As high priced as clothing is today, it's an investment.)

THREE

Organic Synthetic Organic HAIR

————

There are two distinct categories for Black folks' hair. Those categories are "good" or "bad." Black folks today spend thousands of dollars annually, not to mention the number of hours, at beauty salons to maintain "good" hair (even if it isn't organic!).

With the aid of hair care products, the "hairevolution" can be traced back to Madame C. J. Walker, first woman millionaire and entrepreneur extraordinaire, who knew especially what Black women needed for beauty aid and hair care. Madame C. J. Walker (December 23, 1867 to May 25, 1919) made her fortune by developing beauty and hair products for Black women. She developed this interest in a hair tonic to treat her own scalp that had become bald from working with chemicals as a laundress.

Soon afterwards, the Royal Crown hair grease entered the hair care scene, helping the stove-top steaming-hot straightening/pressing comb in its quest to get the kinks out. Soon that which was "organically" straightened through the press-and-curl smoky-house hairdo was inorganically fashioned with the advent of the lye, then no-lye, chemical relaxers (and, lest we forget, the jehri curl). Why in the world would we "press and straighten" our hair in the first place? Why in the world would we put lye, then no-lye, chemicals in our hair? Just doesn't sound natural—maybe there is still an underlying psychology and perhaps issue with being Black and beautiful.

When I think about all of this and recollect my own empirical data, so many questions arise in my mind. One question in particular is which Black-woman self is being presented everyday? Sociologist Erving Goffman would suggest that some Black women's presentation of self is to simply perform on the stage as an affront to the subscribed beauty standard, and it ultimately masks a deeper insecurity and issue with being Black and beautiful. If we could remove the multiple layers of systemic domination, injurious dehumanization, institutionalized racism, blatant sexism, intellectual "down low" (which is the dumbing down of intelligence because others will see you as too much, too qualified, and even too "colored"), and the roles that each have played on the psyche of Sun-kissed Sisters around the world, maybe we could get to the "root" cause of this "hairevolution."

As if the pressing and inorganically straightened hair quest wasn't enough, Black folks, women in particular, got bold with it and started donning the synthetic plastic: wigs, weaves, braids, extensions. Some synthetic and even human hair extensions have been used as a result of hair loss, and some have been used to achieve "good hair." Unfortunately, this is still crippling our Sun-kissed little sisters in post-modernity who should be taught that beauty cannot be bought or bottled. All of this too-much green causes us to lose our natural black. Besides, in the words of my mother, "Pretty is as pretty does." Think about it...

Thank God for liberation and reclamation of the organic root of Black hair and those who dare to be "au natural." Here's a personal story. In a family with three girls, two have "good hair" (Shelia and Angela, my oldest and youngest sisters) and then there was me, smack in the middle of this hair thing. Well, as much of a sacrifice it was, and as hard as it is for me to admit, somebody had to have the brains. Guess that would be me, because I am the natural one!

FOUR

Recycling Food

———

Guess what? Food was recycled, too. And I'm not talking about reheating leftovers. Just read on... Bread ends would be used to make mouth-watering bread pudding. And something called a "dud" loaf was made with fresh butter and sugar—not sure what the dud was other than the "dud" leftover dough from homemade biscuits that wasn't used to make a hoecake. (A hoecake is a huge biscuit that is made from the scraps of leftover dough that my Daddy always got. I used to think that there was something magical, mystical, and masculine about the hoecake until one day I took a bite out of it. It was just like a biscuit, but my Daddy thoroughly enjoyed the otherness nonetheless—just like his daughter, I suppose.)

Oatmeal cooked for breakfast would, later in the day (or week), be transformed into oatmeal cookies. Day-old or week-old cornbread would somehow turn up on the Sunday dinner table as dressing for the chicken after church. Pickle juice would be recycled to pickle boiled eggs. In fact, anything could be pickled if it wasn't eaten soon after the picking. Pickled beets, pickled garlic, pickled onions, pickled pig feet (I'll say more about the pig later, you dig). Grits would turn into a grits casserole. Rice would be recycled into pudding. With a combination of butter, sugar, and nutmeg, Mama could make anything left over into a scrumptious dessert from scratch. And making cakes with Mama was always a treat. Just to be able to crack the eggs and then lick the beaters was enough to brighten any week. (Now we have to worry about salmonella, which sounds like a creepy crawly eight-legged animal.) Nothing was spared, not even the peels of fruits. Daddy could make jelly and preserves out of anything left over! A little "sure gel," sugar, and a mason jar are all it takes. Peach peel preserves is downright decadent and perfect for "sopping up" with a homemade biscuit.

And, yes, you can can. Canning was as much a part of the summer as playing outside. Beware if you had sensitive eyes, because the aroma of vinegar and spices would surely make your eyes burn. Cucumbers to pickles, cabbage to cha-cha (another name for relish), whole pears, tomatoes, okra, too, garlic, even onions and beets would all find their lives extended through winter. Not sure why this was called canning since mason jars were used just like in making jelly.

And for all those who love animals, what greater care than to give your canine your leftovers. Hence the doggie bag would be table scraps, and our mutts (pure bred, of course), named Moon and Mollie, were as healthy as any dog could ever be. No specialized diet, no canine cancer or kidney failures, and they lived long lives for dogs. But wait, not only did dogs get scraps from the kitchen table but if you had hogs, guess what? They did, too! Hence, slopping the hogs literally meant giving the swine the foods left over from the human dine. It was always fun to holler "Sooee" with my paternal grandfather and best friend Papa when it was time to "slop" the hogs.

Speaking of hogs and pigs, there was nothing wasted. From head to tail and all points in between, when a Black person killed a hog, nothing was wasted. From neck bones to pig feet, each had just enough meat to fill you up to work in the heat. Hog mawls (another word for stomach) and hog brains (for breakfast, mixed with eggs) were sure to make you beg for more of this fat meat that sure was greasy. Cholesterol wasn't problematic even with the lard used from the fat meat; just ask Emeril LeGasse. What a great way to season collard greens, turnips, and pinto beans, too.

And, lest we forget, the fragrantly funky flavorful favorites at Christmas, Thanksgiving—anytime would do. Just say chitty-chitty-chitty-bang-bang; to truly appreciate chittlins is a Black thang, no need to try to understand. As grocery stores began to capitalize on what makes Black folks holiday-rize, and as we academized and relished in the bling, we changed chittlins to chitterlings. As Shakespeare would agree, what's in a name? That which we call chitterlings would still stink. It makes no difference whether the name is chittlins or chitterlings, it is a treat to eat.

Hog hoofs were boiled to make tea with its perceived me-dicinal powers (or at least the power in the prayers that healing would take place—simple faith over matter). Hog heads were used to make hog head cheese. (Eaten with saltine crackers, you'd surely be at ease. My dad's trademark souse would cer-tainly please those who would come back for this special snack). Could it be because what humans ate, the hogs ate, and then we ate the hogs and the food chain cycle continued? In other words, you ate what you had eaten. Furthermore, you knew what you ate because you knew what you had eaten.

Just like the hog, the cow's stomach was eaten, too—a nice little meal of tripe. Ride through any inner-city 'hood and you'll see neon signs in lights advertising tripe. Yipes. Ah, but there's more to a cow than its well-known dung; people would even eat the cow's tongue. A delicacy it is, sliced like bologna, baked in aluminum foil, and, oh, the tempting aroma. And would you believe that there was no "mad cow," *E. coli,* or whatever outbreak? Perhaps this is true because we knew what cows ate—just grass, no corn; just grass, no growth hormones; just grass that was green.

Chickens were free range all right. Chickens were "contextually" free to eat the grasshoppers as well as the corn until that glorious day of reckoning (or neck ringing). Dumplings were made with chicken necks and feet; gizzards and livers were not spared but a delicious fried treat. Of course, cooking and frying, baking, too, was all done in cast-iron cookware (even with cooking, there was medicinal help, too). The iron from the cookware would be absorbed into the food; no need for iron supplements because you could add iron activated in the heat of cooking.

Hogs, cows, chickens all coexisting in harmony on the Cooper Farm until that great getting-up day when their lives were sacrificed to feed lives. No one believed these would or could cause harm—let alone *E. coli,* mad cow, salmonella. Produce and herbs grew as well in a magnificent menagerie: greens, tomatoes, spinach, sage, peppermint, blackberries, grapes, crab apples, peaches, pears, black walnuts, plums (best eaten when green—your stomach will say, "you are so mean"). No need to worry because folks knew what they grew. Planting was easy, harvest simple—fruits and veggies you ate while in season. There was no need for international imports of food and no need for disease control because of them. Food was prepared in the home's simple kitchen. No fast food, take-outs, supersizing—just leftovers to recycle for the rest of the week.

Corn cobs were used to make moonshine; actually, let anything ferment and you'd have homemade wine—just ask my brother Gerald! What was not used to eat or drink could easily be converted to some style of decorative pottery.

FIVE

Energy Conservation

———

I know Grandmother Cooper would have a fit to think we have to purchase laundry detergent with the fresh scent of sunshine. Sounds ridiculous, doesn't it. Back in my grandmother's day, clothes were hung on the clothesline. Towels on the front, underwear always in the rear, sheets in the middle was the method for being discreet in displaying the intimate apparel that danced in the wind, sun-kissed to a crisp and air-dried. Those were the days. And there was enough space and no worries about whether someone would steal what was outside and on your property. There was a level of respect; folks kept it real.

As ironic as it may seem, there were not very many folks who had automobiles. No carbon emissions or even pollution. The mode of transportation was with Pat and Bend. Here's how it is explained: "Pat your feet and bend your knees"—folks walked to town (and got exercise, too). For what one couldn't or didn't grow or raise, one would go to the market on Saturdays. My maternal grandmother, Mama Lee (who lived to be almost ninety), was as physically fit as could be and would walk at least five miles to town from Railroad Avenue in Poplar Bluff, Missouri.

SIX

Organic Produce

———

To have a truly authentic and organic garden, here's what you needed to do: Place peels, hulls, cores, and rinds of fruits and vegetables, along with leaves, in a pile—an aromatic compilation for the organic compost (and, of course, you'd attract all the flies). The most natural of natural, no pesticides, herbicides, or hormones were needed to grow the best nuts and the plumpest, juiciest berries.

Aside from the collard greens, turnip greens, and mustard greens that would certainly be requisite, one would always go to the ditch bank (to fish, of course, for catfish) and find growing along the banks "poke" salad. Cook that poke salad with eggs and you talk about "um, um good." Poke salad is just a fancy word for weeds. Wonder why there were no allergies to this weed? Could it be that the immune system was getting an "allergy" shot each time you ate what was organic and in the wild?

There were homegrown and organic remedies found in the garden (just like the hog's hoof tea). Peppermint tea with a bit of local honey would clear up your sinuses and your nose that was runny. A touch of nutmeg on the tongue would clear any stomach ailment. Want to know a cure for a colicky infant? Take off the diaper and dab the tongue—the cure is in the urine. (At least that's what Black folks used to think.)

SEVEN

Concluding Thoughts on Being Black and Green

———

Hope you have learned a bit about the past. Hope we can find ways to reclaim being green and not allow capitalism couched as "bling" to thwart what it means to have, for this day, only what we need.

To be green we must first rid ourselves of plastic, and that includes toothbrushes, drinking straws, credit cards, medicine bottles, polyester, rayon, credit cards, garbage cans, syringes, disposable diapers, credit cards, blinds, shades, ice trays, credit cards, plastic training pants, computers, gift cards (what a waste), telephones, cars, churches, credit cards, schools, houses, bandages, hospitals, movie theaters, credit cards, poker chips, casinos, toys, baby bottles, credit cards, restaurants, governments, false teeth, credit cards—need I go on?

Hindsight is always twenty-twenty. I wish I had taken seriously my mother's frugality and my father's advice. Daddy would say, if you don't have the cash to pay for it, you don't need it. Like many college students who were coming of age and especially with the temptation of giving organizations a percentage of proceeds from new credit applications, I was suckerpunched into the realm of debt. I was bigger than life and arrogant to boot. I dared the companies to give me a credit card, especially since I wrote I didn't have an income on the application. But for each one that I received, I figured those places were stupid, when in fact I was the uneducated moron. I was the one who purchased step show outfits, books, food, as I "Discovered" my way into debt. There was nothing Famous at the Barr nor any Capital for One, just an additive cycle of creating debt. The tragedy is I had every intention of paying the first bill, but soon it was too deep. Too much plastic hovering around my life until I found myself drowning in the plastic debt. A word to the Nintendo Generation: Don't do the credit till you have an income. In fact, do what your grandparents did, pay with cash, please. Sustainable living is obtainable if you live within your means.

We don't need much, just food, clothing, and a place to lay our heads. If you see your neighbor struggling, give a thought to include her at your table. Show love to each, especially the other. If you want to walk or ride a bike, eat meat or veggies—that's all right. Can we just live and let each of us be good stewards of this Earth? It's up to you, Nintendo Generation, to reclaim the roots, not be mean, when others don't seem to get why it's not easy being green. Sustainable living is obtainable when we live within our means.

EASY WAYS TO BE GREEN

1. Turn off the television and talk. Share your wisdom with your children so that they can pass on stories to the next generation. The time that you spend with a young person is priceless.

2. Wash dishes. If you find yourself relying too much on paper plates and plastic forks (or, heaven forbid, Styrofoam), take time now to start ridding your kitchen space of these nobio-degradable items.

3. Cloth napkins are not only sensible but elegant as well. You may even teach your child how to eat in a formal dining room setting. (How about it?)

4. Plant a garden and use compost from peels, rinds, and leaves as natural fertilizer. You can also use seeds from certain fruits and vegetables to get it started at a low cost.

5. Plant a tree, especially modeling the trees planted on the Cooper Farm. If you have a yard with lots of trees, be neighborly and share the seedlings.

6. Read, write, and even fly a kite!

7. Encourage outside activities to foster imaginative play that will spill over even on rainy days.

8. Walk or ride a bike, for both exercise and as a way to reduce your carbon footprint.

9. Turn off lights when the space is not being used (even if you're at work or at school).

10. Convert plastic bags into reusable, sturdy handbags to do grocery shopping, carry books, and lots more. You can find out how by looking on YouTube for the "Trash Bags to Hand Bags How-To" provided by the Roots and Shoots organization at Doane College, or you can follow the simple steps below:

    A. Gather up all your disposable plastic grocery and shopping bags.

    B. Turn them inside out and cut off the handles and the seam along the bottom so you have a nice, flat item with two openings.

    C. Put a piece of wax paper down on the ironing board, tabletop, or whatever.

    D. Lay four of your plastic bags on top of the wax paper. You want four bags because you need to make it eight-ply to properly melt. Lay another piece of wax paper over the top, like a sandwich. Make sure your wax paper hangs out over the ends of the plastic bags.

E. With a slightly warm iron, probably set for rayon or poly-
    ester, iron over the wax paper, pressing down enough
    that you literally melt the plastic bags together under
    the wax paper. BE CAREFUL that the plastic does not
    touch the iron.

F. After ironing one side, flip it over and repeat so that both
    sides are thoroughly melted together. You can tell it is
    perfect if the plastic no longer moves. It should be one
    solid piece.

G. Repeat this whole process so that you now have two nice
    pieces of sturdy material for sewing.

H. Cut yourself a piece of cardboard for a template that
    looks like this:

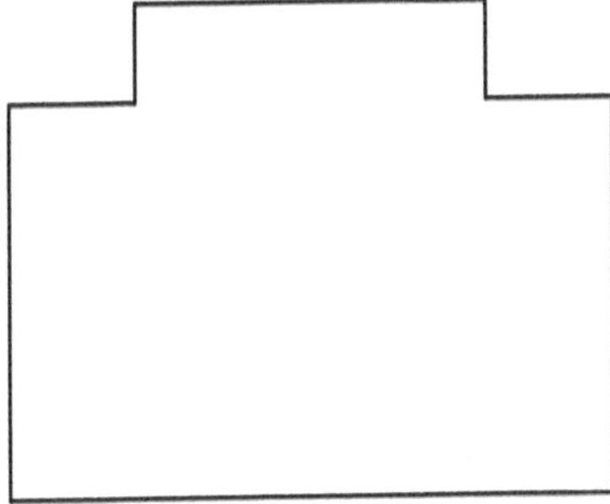

I. Use your template as a pattern: Lay it down on your two pieces of material and trace around it.

J. Cut around the lines on your material so that you now have two pieces of material ready to sew together that look like this:

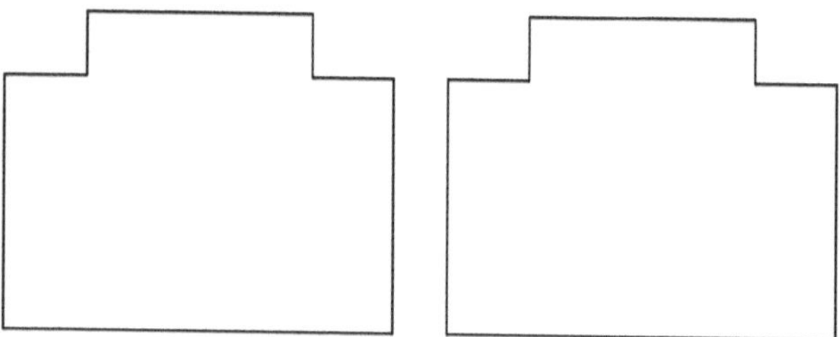

K. You are ready to sew the two pieces together. Put the two pieces together and sew the bottom of the two "flaps" together first.

L. After you have sewn all the sides together, your bag should look like this:

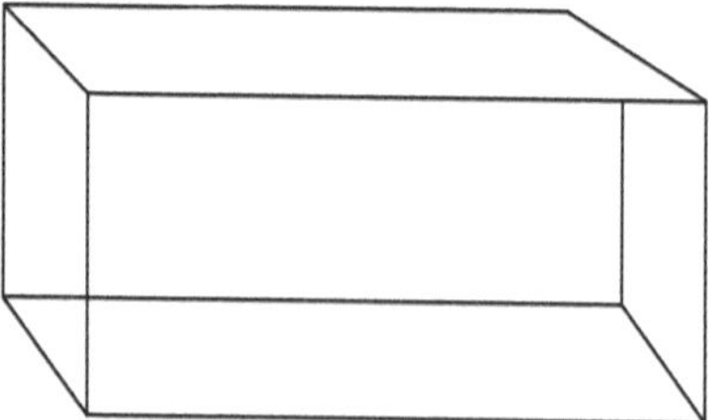

M. Now you need to melt together some more plastic
(remember, make it eight-ply) and cut yourself some
straps—you will need four of equal length.

M. Sew the four straps to the front and back side of the bag
like this:

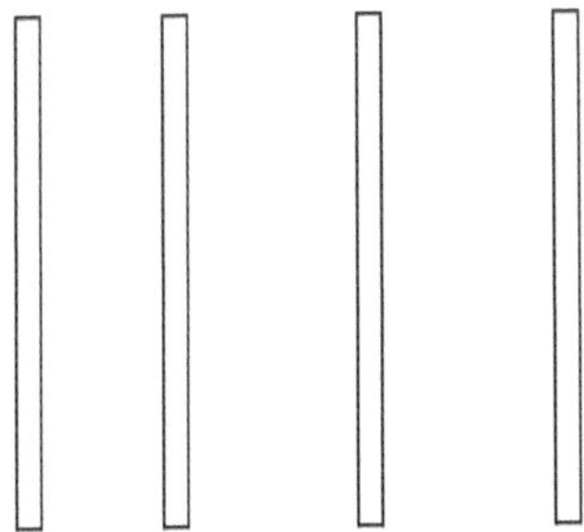

O. Now you can sew the handles together. If you want
a really sturdy bag, make the straps long enough that
they reach under the bottom of the bag and come up
again on the opposite side. This will help support the
bottom.

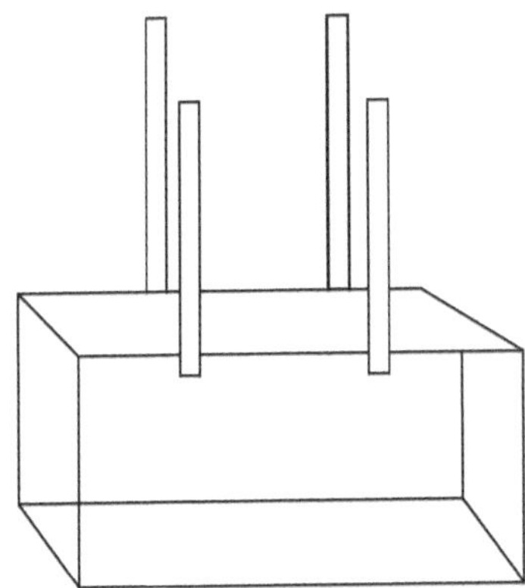

P. Now go fill that bag every time you shop and never throw it away!

11. Be nice to spiders, for they have a place in the ecological system, along with other insects. Use natural pesticides if bugs bug you. Marigolds are a great way to keep mosquitoes away.

12. Love your neighbor as you love yourself.

And Man created the plastic bag and the tin and aluminum
can and the cellophane wrapper and the paper plate and the
disposable bottle, and this was good because Man could then
take his automobile and buy his food all in one place and he
could save that which was good to eat in the refrigerator and
throw away that which had no further use. And pretty soon the
earth was covered with plastic bags and aluminum cans and
paper plates and disposable bottles, and there was nowhere
left to sit down or to walk. And Man shook his head and cried,
"Look at all this God-awful litter."

—*Art Buchwald, 1970*

Left to right: Grandmother Cooper, Mrs. West, Aunt Bobbye, Miss Ozzie Ruff, my mother Kay, Aunt Lorraine Sims.

Seated: John Cooper, Earnest Cooper, Roy Cooper Sr. (Papa).
Standing: Uncle Robert Sims.

Great-Grandmother Mama Black.

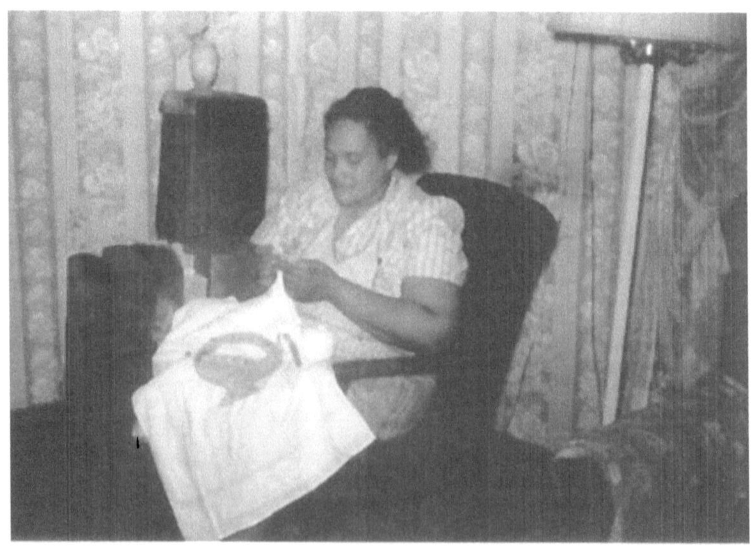

Grandmother quilting, one of her favorite pastimes.

My dad, Joel Curtis Cooper, at the pit for the reunion.

Photo of the Cooper Farm today.

My grandmother Louise Cooper in the Gardening Magazine *cover photo.*

The FARM HOME

Frida Schulthess
WOMAN'S EDITOR

PROGRESS has been notable since the Roy Cooper family purchased a 160-acre farm in 1939 with the help of a loan from the Farmers Home administration.

Their land, lying two and a half miles northeast of Pascola, in Pemiscot County, Missouri, is operated along with a nearby rented 40-acre tract.

An Active Family.

The Coopers have been local-place Missouri winners in the landowner division of the Live-At-Home campaign. They have built a home served with running water. A bathroom has been a much appreciated addition. There is an electric range in their kitchen and a freezer in their utility room. Mrs. Ella Stackhouse, Negro home agent for Dunklin-Pemiscot Counties, counseled in the planning of their home.

The farm land is mostly in soybeans, wheat and cotton. Two cows to keep the family supplied with milk, chickens and hogs to maintain the family's needs for meat and eggs, account for the family livestock.

Four sons of the Negro family—Roy, Maginth, Charles and Alex were graduated from Lincoln university, Jefferson City. Roy and Alex, who have been instructors in Missouri schools, will continue their teaching careers. Charles is hopeful for a career in medicine and attending Meharry university, Nashville, Tenn.

A Football Player.

Joel, another son, left the university early this year to play professional football with the Denver Bears, but plans required studies at Lincoln university for a bachelor of science degree.

Melvin, who studied at Lincoln, is now at a vocational school at Paducah, Ky. Maginth, after graduating from Lincoln last spring, became employed at an aircraft industry in Wichita.

Still at home is Thomas, 13. The one girl in the family, Jewel, is a student at Central high school, Hayti. She is ambitious to become a laboratory worker. John, 23, was fatally injured in an automobile accident last May, shortly after completing army training.

All the brothers have helped finance each other through school.

The Coopers are well along toward fulfilling plans for landscaping their farmstead. Their living room is graced by many house plants. During the last several months when Mrs. Cooper required respite from the most strenuous kinds of housework, she has devoted much time ...

Theirs Is a Record of Progress.

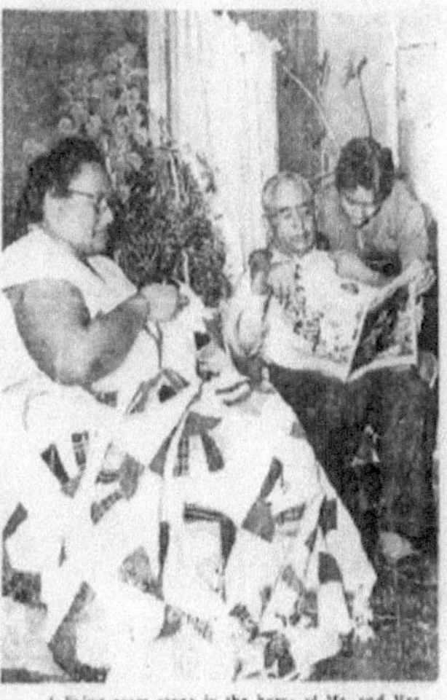

A living room scene in the home of Mr. and Mrs. Roy Cooper, a Negro family living on a farm near Pascola, Pemiscot County, Missouri. Jewel, a daughter, shares the magazine her father is reading. Mrs. Cooper is engaged with putting together a quilt, Grandmother's Fan.

A home of their own has been constructed by the Coopers. Next on the program of improvement will be landscaping their farmstead.

MO   WEEKLY

The Rural

STAR FARMER, WEDNESDAY, AUGUST 3, 1960.

Homemaker

One of many news articles about my grandparents and their children.

Offspring of Alex Cooper and Mary Perteet. Roy Cooper Sr., my grandfather, is standing third from the left.

ABOUT THE AUTHOR

The Rev. Karla J. Cooper, EdD, the seventh child of eight children of Joel and Kay Cooper, is ordained as an itinerant elder of the African Methodist Episcopal Church, currently serving Allen-St. John AME Church in Kansas City after a fourteen-year pastoral appointment in Lincoln, Nebraska, serving the Historical Quinn Chapel AME Church. She served with distinction as chaplain/coordinator of service programs at Doane University for ten years. She is currently associate professor of practice in the College of Education at Doane. She is also adjunct faculty with Nebraska Wesleyan University in the Department of Sociology. She has taught courses in service learning and cultural immersion in India for Doane since 2011 and has led various delegations to India since her first trip in 2003. From this experience, her students have achieved various pursuits, including a Fullbright scholar to India, Peace Corps volunteer to Liberia, and Stanford University program adviser for the Bing Overseas Studies Program, just to name a few.

More importantly, the African Methodist Episcopal Church has a presence on the continent of Asia with more than 160 churches and two Presiding Elder Districts because of a literal dream that Dr. Cooper had one night and shared in 2004 with Bishop John Bryant and Rev. Cecelia Williams Bryant, former bishop and supervisor of the 5th Episcopal District. Dr. Cooper often shares that her first trip to India in 2003 was so overwhelming that she was unable to talk about it for an entire year. Equally, the trip was transformative not only in her life but expanded the global witness and ministry of the AME church nearly one hundred years after the church first expanded on the continent of Africa.

Because Lincoln, Nebraska, is a sanctuary city and the state of Nebraska has the second-largest population of Sudanese outside of the Sudan, Dr. Cooper has informed the minds of many students from South Sudan, Afghanistan, Iraq, Iran, Liberia, Nigeria, and Guatemala. Dr. Cooper partnered with Jesus LaRoca, where Pastor Martha Rodriquez serves as founder and senior pastor, to offer space for worship and Bible study for the Spanish-speaking community. She is a visiting lecturer at Kenya Methodist University and pastoral trainer for Bishop Catherine Mutua, presiding bishop from the Kaaga Synod in Meru, Kenya. She has also lectured at Madras Christian College in Chennai, India.

She is a graduate of Eden Theological Seminary, where she received a master of divinity and studied abroad as part of a 2003 travel seminar to India, studying in three seminaries: Gurukul Lutheran Theological Seminary in Chennai, Tamilnadu Theological Seminary, and United Theological Seminary in Bangalore. She holds a doctorate in education, EdD, from Doane University and has credentialed herself with studies in sociology from the University of Nebraska as a former PhD student. Dr. Cooper's research is on the intersectionality of race, gender, class, religion, and sexual orientation with a particular focus on the transgender community.

Dr. Cooper serves on the board of trustees for Eden Theological Seminary. She has served in various capacities throughout the State of Missouri. She has been a gubernatorial appointee under both Gov. Carnahan and Gov. Holden, working on issues such as National and Community Services, the Senior Prescription Drug Policy Task Force, and a Systems Reform Initiative called Caring Communities. Dr. Cooper has also worked with former Secretary of State Colin Powell with the America's Promise Initiative. She gained national recognition from the Ford Foundation and Harvard University for her work with welfare reform, and she created the alternative school DREAMERS and the youth diversion initiative PASSAGES.

Dr. Cooper is a former connectional officer with Women In Ministry of the African Methodist Episcopal Church, serving as financial secretary for 2008–09, is dean of the Board of Examiners Midwest Annual Conference, and serves on the Conference Trustees of the Midwest Annual Conference.

Cooper has served on many boards and commissions, including Girl Scouts, Cotton Boll Council and Homestead Council; Bootheel Heart Health Coalition; Minority Health Initiative; Fresh Start board; Delta Sigma Theta national executive board/ central regional director. She has served on the Lincoln Commission on Human Rights and the Interfaith Worker Justice Commission. She also served on the Foundation for Lincoln Public Schools, one of the top ten public school systems in the US with a large number of refugees and first-time US citizens from Arabic- and Spanish-speaking countries.

Dr. Cooper is the immediate past president of the Mary Riepma Ross Theater Board that managed an endowment of more than $10 million. She has served on the Family Violence Council Board and the Parents and Friends of Lesbians and Gays (PFLAG) board, where she was editor of the monthly newsletter.

In 2009, the Women's Global Initiative awarded Cooper with an ecological justice award during a convocation in Toronto, Canada, for being the first Black woman to write a book on ecology. She was featured along with the late Dr. Wangari Maathai, the 2004 Nobel Peace Prize winner known for her contribution to sustainable development, democracy, and peace, as founder of the Greenbelt Movement in Kenya.

Dr. Cooper is the author of *When Blacks Were Green*, published by Infusionmedia, and is coauthor of the chapter "Where Race, Gender and Orientation Meet" with Dr. Joretta Marshall in the pastoral care manual *Volume IV: Women out of Order: Risking Change and Creating Care in a Multicultural World*, published by Fortress Press.

She is a much sought-after speaker on issues of child advocacy, public policy, systems reform, and cultural diversity.

www.ingramcontent.com/pod-product-compliance
Lightning Source LLC
Chambersburg PA
CBHW030824060726
47590CB00004B/1392